Rebecca Gordine

50

fantastic ideas for
supporting children's wellbeing

FEATHERSTONE

FEATHERSTONE
Bloomsbury Publishing Plc
50 Bedford Square, London, WC1B 3DP, UK

BLOOMSBURY, FEATHERSTONE and the Feather logo are trademarks of Bloomsbury Publishing Plc

First published in Great Britain 2020 by Bloomsbury Publishing Plc

A catalogue record for this book is available from the British Library

ISBN: PB: 978-1-4729-6676-6; ePDF: 978-1-4729-6677-3

2 4 6 8 10 9 7 5 3 1

Series design: Lynda Murray

Printed and bound in India by Replika Press Pvt. Ltd.

MIX
Paper from
responsible sources
FSC® C016779

To find out more about our authors and books visit www.bloomsbury.com and sign up for our newsletters

Acknowledgements

I would like to thank Logan Gray for taking the beautiful photographs for this book and Nevill Road
Infant School for allowing the use of the school grounds.

Contents

Introduction

What is wellbeing?

For anyone working with young children, an understanding of how to support and develop their emotional and physical wellbeing is of great importance. If children feel calm, relaxed and comfortable in their environment and comfortable with their peers and the adults around them, they will be able to play, learn and develop successfully. Feelings of wellbeing, whether physical or emotional, can boost self-confidence and independence.

It is good practice, in Early Years settings, to encourage children to take time to be calm, quiet and thoughtful. By teaching children the basic principles of mindfulness and relaxation, we are providing them with the tools they need as they grow up to protect their physical, emotional and mental health.

How can this book support children's wellbeing?

The activities in this book have been carefully chosen for use with young children and will support them in developing a sense of wellbeing. As well as helping children to feel happiness and joy, many of the activities also facilitate the development of positive relationships with other children and adults – improving their social skills and friendships.

Many of the activities in this book incorporate, in some way, nature and the outdoors. It has been proved that spending time outside with nature raises 'feel good' hormones and fosters a greater sense of wellbeing and happiness. Learning about nature, about plants, animals, weather and the environment helps children to understand the world in which they live as well as learning about how to care for their environment and the wider world. Children learn the values of kindness, gentleness and empathy through interactions with nature. Physical activity and movement is good for overall health and wellbeing. It is a good idea to try to incorporate as much outdoor time as possible when caring for, and teaching, young children.

Practical activities, where children are involved in 'hands on' experiences, develop feelings of satisfaction and achievement in children. Making and creating are sensory activities which can be calming and relaxing for children and adults alike, and they also foster a sense of belonging and comfort. Sometimes, the conversations had with children while they are engaged in a creative activity can be the most interesting and rewarding ones as children are able to relax and express themselves and their ideas freely.

Who will benefit from this book?

This book is written for anyone caring for, or working with young children, who is interested in nurturing their emotional, mental and physical wellbeing. The activities have been designed and chosen for the feelings of togetherness, calmness and happiness that they create.

The structure of the book

Before you start any activity, read through everything on the page so you are familiar with the whole activity and what you might need to plan in advance. The pages are all organised in the same way.

What you need lists the resources required for the activity. These are likely to be readily available in most settings or can be bought or made easily.

What to do tells you step by step what you need to do to complete the activity.

Top tips give a brief word of advice or helpful tip that could make all the difference to the experience of the activity for you and your children.

The **Health & Safety** tips are often obvious, but safety can't be overstressed. In many cases there are no specific hazards involved in completing the activity, and your usual health and safety measures should be enough. In others there are particular issues to be noted and addressed.

What's in it for the children? tells you (and others) briefly how the suggested activities contribute to learning.

Taking it forward gives ideas for additional activities on the same theme, or for developing the activity further. These will be particularly useful for things that have gone especially well or where children show a real interest. In many cases they use the same resources, and in every case they have been designed to extend learning and broaden the children's experiences.

Finally, **Observation questions** prompt the practitioner to evaluate how the children are engaging with one another and the activity itself, with links to the EYFS Statutory Framework.

Super soup

A warm and comforting food to share with friends

What you need:

- Tuff tray
- Antibacterial spray
- Chopping boards
- Knives
- Onions
- Potatoes
- Leeks
- Carrots
- Pan
- Vegetable stock
- Wooden spoon
- Hand blender
- Bread

What's in it for the children?

Children enjoy helping grown ups in the kitchen and they will like making soup that they can all enjoy together. Learning how to chop vegetables safely is an important life skill. By preparing and cooking the soup themselves, children feel a sense of pride and satisfaction. Sharing food and eating it with others fosters happiness, togetherness and friendship, all of which contribute to wellbeing.

Taking it forward

- Children could make recipe cards with picture instructions for their friends to follow.
- They could learn how to cook other recipes too.

Observation questions

- Can children follow instructions?
- Do children know the rules for safe chopping?
- Can children talk about healthy food?

What to do:

1. Working with a small group of children, talk about any cooking they have done in the past. Do they help their parents or carers cook at home?

2. Clean a tuff tray thoroughly using antibacterial spray and set out the chopping boards. Invite the children to wash their hands thoroughly and talk about food safety.

3. Discuss knife safety and rules before you begin. Model how to chop the vegetables safely. Help the children to chop the onions, potatoes, leeks and carrots into small chunks. You may need to pre-chop or peel some of the vegetables first.

4. Transfer all of the vegetables to a pan and cover with vegetable stock. Season if required.

5. Cook on a medium heat until all the vegetables have softened. Allow the children to take turns stirring the pan carefully.

6. Blend the soup with a hand blender.

7. Provide bread and allow the children to enjoy their soup with their friends.

✚ Health & Safety

Check for any food allergies before you start the activity.

Den making
Build a social space

What you need:

- Space, outdoor or indoor
- Blanket or fabric
- Pegs
- Rug
- Soft furnishings, e.g. cushions, throws and blankets
- Books
- Teddies or favourite toys
- Torch

What's in it for the children?

Den making is a fun activity for young children. They can use their problem-solving and negotiating skills as they work as a team to create a useable den. Children must work as a team, using each other's strengths to solve problems as they go and to make a practical, functional space. The physical activity, the social activity, as well as the feeling of accomplishment when it is finished all contribute to a child's overall sense of wellbeing.

Taking it forward

- Make signs for the den.
- Make more complex dens with separate rooms and a garden.
- Make dens for wildlife to visit.

Observation questions

- Can children work as part of a team?
- Can children adapt their ideas as they go?
- Can children talk about their ideas?

What to do:

1. Ask the children if they have ever built a den before. Ask them to tell you about their best dens. What makes a good den? How many people should fit inside? Who would they invite into their den?

2. Work with the children to find a place, inside or outside, to build a den. If inside, under a table or between two chairs can work well. If outside, near a tree or other structure is a good den space.

3. Help the children to cover over the den space with a blanket or large piece of fabric. You may need to use giant pegs to secure it. Ensure any bits at the side or back are covered.

4. Cover the floor or ground inside the den with a rug.

5. Invite the children to fill the den with cushions and other soft furnishings to make it feel cosy.

6. Suggest that they include books, teddies and other favourite toys in the space.

7. Provide torches and allow the children to explore the den space.

Hug a friend

Build trust and security

What you need:

- A friend

What's in it for the children?

Hugging is powerful in its ability to make others feel loved and cared for. Hugs build trust and a feeling of safety. Hugging can help children sooth their fears and worries and it helps them feel connected to others. Hugging releases oxytocin which relaxes and calms both the person who initiated the hug and the person being hugged.

Taking it forward

- Children could have a special seat or area where they can go if they need a hug. This space could have cushions and soft toys.

- Discussion could be opened up about whether people in history used to hug each other and why people do it in the first place.

Observation questions

- Do children like hugging?

- Can children talk about how hugs and touch make them feel?

What to do:

1. Talk to the children about hugging. Use these questions to prompt discussion:
   a. How do you feel when you hug someone?
   b. Do you like to hug?
   c. Did people a long time ago hug each other?
   d. Do animals hug each other?

2. Invite the children to pair up with a friend and give them a big friendly hug.

3. Get the children into a circle and ask them to pass a hug around the circle. Children have to remain focussed and maintain attention so that they are ready for when the hug comes round to them.

4. Talk about how they felt when they were hugged. How did they feel when they hugged someone else?

5. Another game would be to make a circle and one child stands in the middle with their eyes closed. Another child from the circle is chosen to quietly approach the middle child and hug them, then run quickly back to their place. The child in the middle opens their eyes and has to guess who hugged them.

Movie time

Relax and enjoy time with friends

What you need:

- Popcorn
- Microwave
- A selection of feel-good films
- Blankets and cushions

What to do:

1. Make some popcorn in the microwave with the children. Follow any instructions on the packet.

2. Discuss the children's favourite films. Decide together which film to watch.

3. Set out blankets and cushions. Encourage children to snuggle with their friends under a blanket and enjoy the film together. Share the popcorn.

4. After the film, prompt the children with questions such as 'What was the film about?', 'Who were the main characters?' and 'What did you like or dislike about it?'.

5. Talk about how nice it is to watch a film together.

✚ Health & Safety

Check for any food allergies before you start the activity.

What's in it for the children?

Shared experiences such as watching a film together with friends or family are important for young children to develop a sense of belonging. Sitting down and watching a film is relaxing and calming for the mind and body. Sitting still and letting their body relax is important for children who, generally, lead very active lives.

Taking it forward

- Children could prepare for the film by making cinema tickets for their friends.

- They could arrange the furniture so that it looks like a cinema.

- Children could give a review at the end of the film, talking about why they liked or disliked it.

Observation questions

- Can children listen and maintain attention for the duration of the film?

- Can children talk about what they have watched?

- Can they talk about why they like or dislike the film?

Baking cookies

Evoke happy feelings and memories through baking

What you need:

- Cookie ingredients
    - 125 g butter (room temperature)
    - 100 g brown sugar
    - 1 egg
    - 1½ tsp vanilla essence
    - ½ tsp salt
    - 225 g self-raising flour
    - 200 g chocolate chips
- Mixing bowl
- Mixing spoon or spatula
- Baking tray
- Baking parchment
- Oven gloves
- Oven

What to do:

1. Discuss the children's favourite cookies. What do they think goes into cookies? Have they ever made them before?

2. Gather the ingredients and equipment you need. The basic ingredients are listed in the 'What you need' section.

3. Pre-heat the oven to 200°C.

4. Mix the butter and sugar in a large bowl. Allow the children to take turns. Is the mixture hard to stir?

5. Add the egg and vanilla essence and mix again.

6. Pour in the salt and flour and combine well. Ask the children how the mixture feels now. What does it smell like? What is happening to the mixture?

7. Add the chocolate chips and mix. The mixture will now be quite stiff.

8. Line a baking tray with baking parchment and roll the mixture into little balls. Place these on the baking tray.

9. Use oven gloves to carefully put the cookies into the oven for 7–10 minutes until they are cooked.

10. As the cookies bake, ask the children what they can smell. Is it a pleasant smell? Does it evoke any memories for them?

11. Let the cookies cool and then enjoy!

➕ **Health & Safety**

Check for any food allergies before you start the activity.

What's in it for the children?

Most children love to bake with a grown up and this is a wonderful wellbeing activity. They enjoy being able to mix the ingredients to make something which can be eaten and enjoyed by everyone. Following a recipe can calm the mind as it requires concentration on the task. Cookies are a comfort food and the smell and taste of them can create a sense of wellbeing.

Taking it forward

- Bake different recipes of various complexity.

- Invite children to create their own recipes.

- Ask children to decorate boxes for their cookies and deliver the treats to friends, relatives or neighbours to brighten someone's day.

Observation questions

- Can children follow instructions?

- Can children predict what will happen?

- Can children talk about changes?

- Can children talk about smell, touch and taste?

Pet's corner

Feeling a connection with other living things

What you need:

- Time to visit a petting farm

What's in it for the children?

Stroking pets and animals is soothing and most animals like it too! Touch is powerful; it can make people feel loved and cherished. Stroking a pet or animal also has a calming effect on children and the feeling of connection between animal and child can support their feeling of wellbeing.

Taking it forward

- Children could stroke a variety of different animals and talk about the textures of their fur.
- Discussion can be opened up about animals and habitats.

Observation questions

- Can children talk about how animals make them feel?
- Can they talk about their favourite animal?
- Can they describe different textures?

✚ Health & Safety

Check for any pet allergies before you start the activity.

What to do:

1. As part of a topic on animals or farming, arrange for the children to visit a petting farm.

2. Before the visit, discuss whether the children have any pets at home and how it feels to interact with them.

3. During the visit, remind children to ask for permission to stroke the animals. Model the repetitive action of stroking and discuss how this is soothing for you and the animal. Explain that by stroking an animal's fur you are caring for it and it feels good to care for others.

4. Ensure children wash their hands with soap and water after the session.

Snuggling with a hot chocolate

Share a cosy space with friends

What you need:

- Hot chocolate powder
- Pan
- Milk or water
- Jug
- Wooden spoon
- Blankets
- Cushions
- Cups

What's in it for the children?

This simple activity involves sharing a cosy space and enjoying it together. The warm drink and the blanket, as well as snuggling up with someone special, creates a feeling of comfort and wellbeing for all involved as it helps them to feel safe and protected.

Taking it forward

- Children could be supported in making different kinds of drinks.
- Children could be given the responsibility of making drinks for their friends at snack time.
- Twinkly lights, a bubble lamp or dimming the lights would enhance the experience further.

Observation questions

- Do children enjoy quiet, calm time?
- Can children engage in conversation with others?

Health & Safety

Check for any food allergies before you start the activity.

What to do:

1. Invite a small group of children to make hot chocolate with you.
2. Talk to them about those times when a hug and a snuggle can help them to feel better.
3. Follow the instructions on the hot chocolate packet. Pour the hot chocolate powder into a pan.
4. Help the children to measure the correct volume of milk or water in a jug and carefully pour it into the pan with the powder. Invite the children to take turns stirring the mixture with a wooden spoon.
5. On a low heat, slowly warm up the hot chocolate while the children find a cosy place to sit. Provide them with blankets and cushions so they can make the space inviting.
6. When the drink is ready, pour it into cups and sit with the children as they drink. Encourage them to talk about how being warm and cosy makes them feel.

Nature walk

A feel-good activity, whatever the weather

What you need:

- Weather-appropriate clothing, e.g. wellies
- Camera

What to do:

1. Make sure every child has appropriate clothes for the weather. Ask the children about the weather – is it warm or cold today?

2. Tell the children that you will be taking a nature walk together. Build excitement by discussing all of the wonderful and interesting things they hope to see, touch, smell and hear. Encourage them to think about how the outdoors makes them feel.

3. Set off on a nature walk.

4. Listen out for sounds and watch out for wildlife. Talk about how relaxing it is to be outside.

5. Encourage them to take photographs of what they can see as they walk, especially any natural objects or textures that they enjoy.

What's in it for the children?

This feel-good activity is good for the body as it is exercise in the fresh air. It is good for the mind because children are encouraged to focus on their senses – what they can hear, see, touch and smell.

Taking it forward

- Children could have a tick list of things they might spot and they could tick them off as they go along.

- Children could create a picture or collage of their walk when they get back.

Observation questions

- Can children use their senses to explore their surroundings?

- Can children talk about the things they have seen and heard?

Cutting straws

Developing strength and competence with fine motor skills

What you need:

- Paper straws in various sizes, colours and patterns
- Scissors
- Table top or tuff tray

What to do:

1. Set out the straws and scissors on an accessible table top or tuff tray. Make sure you have a variety of sizes of straw and left-handed scissors if required.

2. Encourage the children to use the scissors to cut the straws into pieces of varying lengths.

3. Suggest that they might change the angle of the cut or cut through the length of the straw to make a flat piece.

4. If your straws have patterns, e.g. stripes, suggest that the children could cut along the patterns.

5. Allow them to access the activity for as long as they like.

What's in it for the children?

Learning to use scissors independently, competently and safely is an important skill in the early years. Cutting straws is a fun activity for children which develops their scissor skills, concentration and their physical wellbeing. Mastering a skill also increases children's sense of accomplishment and emotional wellbeing.

Taking it forward

- Children could make a collage using the bits of straws they have cut up.

- They could order the straw pieces from shortest to tallest.

Observation questions

- Can children use scissors independently, competently and safely?

- Do children know how to hold and carry scissors safely?

Body awareness

Develop concentration and awareness of the body

What you need:

- Comfortable chairs or mats

What's in it for the children?

This activity encourages children to be still and quiet and to relax for a moment. It encourages children to focus on each part of their body and how it feels. This will calm and soothe children. By tensing and relaxing each muscle, children become more aware of what happens to their body if they feel worried, angry or frustrated. By concentrating on the task, children will not be focussing on worries or negative thoughts.

Taking it forward

- Include this activity as part of your daily schedule.
- Children could use this strategy independently to calm down if they are feeling angry, worried or frustrated.
- Encourage children to teach their friends how to do it.

Observation questions

- Can children be quiet and concentrate for a 15-minute period?
- Are children able to use this skill to calm themselves if they are cross or frustrated?
- Can children talk about how their body feels?

What to do:

1. Discuss how it feels when you are angry, worried or frustrated. Demonstrate how sometimes people will squeeze their hands into fists when this happens. Ask the children to practise squeezing their hands in this way, then releasing. Discuss the 'release' sensation.

2. Invite the children to sit in a comfortable chair or lay on a mat on the floor.

3. Ask them to close their eyes and take long deep breaths for a minute.

4. Starting at the head, tune in to how your head feels at that particular time by thinking of how the top of your head feels, how your face feels and how heavy it feels.

5. Tense your head by squeezing your eyes and jaw tightly, hold for three seconds and relax.

6. Repeat this tense-and-relax sequence for each part of the body, e.g. shoulders, arms, bottom, thighs, and so on.

7. Once the activity is complete, ask children to return to a sitting position (if they were laying down) and ask them how they feel. How does each part of their body feel? Do they feel relaxed?

Parachute

Listen, concentrate and follow instructions

What you need:

- Parachute
- A large space
- Soft balls of different sizes

What to do:

1. Discuss what it's like to work in a team. What makes a good team member?

2. Spread a parachute out on the ground (you will need a large space for this).

3. Get a group of children to stand around the edge of the parachute, holding on to the edges.

4. Place some soft balls on top of the parachute.

5. Ask children to softly move the parachute up and down, causing the balls to bounce. This should be a gentle, teamwork activity so the balls shouldn't bounce too high. Encourage them to work together so that the balls don't fall.

What's in it for the children?

In this game, children have to concentrate on the activity to prevent the balls from falling off the parachute. They have to listen to instructions and follow them. They are developing their listening, attention and understanding skills. They also need to work as a team. Teamwork and having fun with friends leads to a feeling of wellbeing as part of a group.

Taking it forward

- Children could swap places under the parachute when it is lifted if they have a particular trait, e.g. blue eyes, brown hair, their name begins with 'A'.
- Children could invent their own parachute game.

Observation questions

- Can children concentrate on the activity?
- Can children follow instructions?
- Can children make up their own game?

Rainmaker
What sounds can you hear?

What you need:

- Cardboard tubes, enough for one each
- Paint
- Felt-tip pens
- Clear sticky tape
- Rice, dry lentils or beans

Top tip ⭐

Ensure the rainmakers are secured with sticky tape before allowing the children to use them to reduce the choking risk caused by small pieces such as dried beans.

What's in it for the children?

Making music brings happiness. Making your own instrument brings satisfaction and pride too. Music encourages children to dance, move and sing, all of which support contentment and enjoyment. Listening to, and making music, is enjoyable and can bring children together to dance and sing. Moving your body and physical activity also contribute to overall wellbeing.

Taking it forward

- Children could make a range of different instruments.
- A group of children may like to form their own band, encouraging teamwork and collaboration.

Observation questions

- Can children make instruments?
- Can children move, dance, make music and sing?
- Can children describe the sounds they hear?

What to do:

1. Talk to the children about their favourite songs and rhymes. Do they like listening to or making music?
2. Give each child a cardboard tube. Allow them time to decorate it using paints or felt-tip pens.
3. Seal one end of the tube with a cardboard circle and clear sticky tape.
4. Add rice, dry lentils or beans.
5. Secure the open end of the cardboard tube with more cardboard and tape.
6. Shake your rainmaker!

Rainy day puddle fun

Endless fun outdoors to promote physical wellbeing

What you need:

- Old clothing or a change of clothing
- Wellies
- Puddles
- Paint

What to do:

1. Choose a day when there has already been a lot of rain but it is not too cold. Ensure the children are appropriately dressed in old clothes and suggest that parents provide a change of clothes in case anyone gets very wet.

2. Invite the children to put their wellies on.

3. Allow them to go outside and encourage them to find a big puddle.

4. Suggest that they could splash and jump in the puddles, watching to see what happens to the water.

5. Add powder paint to the puddle and see what happens.

What's in it for the children?

Most children enjoy splashing in puddles. It is fun to watch the water move and to hear the sound of splashing. Adding paint to the puddles creates patterns. Jumping is active, it gets the heart pumping and it gets the endorphins flowing – all of which are good for children's physical wellbeing.

Taking it forward

- Children could splash in other liquids or substances and see what happens, e.g. shaving foam, mud, slime, icing sugar.

- Children could add paint or ink to other materials and talk about how this changes the water and the splash patterns it creates.

Observation questions

- Do children enjoy jumping in puddles?

- Can they make patterns and talk about changes?

- Can children talk about how jumping makes them feel?

Rolling down a hill

Fun with friends in the great outdoors

What you need:

- A gentle slope
- Tarpaulin sheet (optional)

What's in it for the children?

Rolling down a hill is fun. It is exhilarating. Children will enjoy this activity, especially if they do it with friends too. The physical activity of rolling is fun, it makes children smile and laugh. Laughter and making memories with friends is good for children's wellbeing.

Taking it forward

- Children could discuss how fast or slow they would roll down a steeper or flatter slope.

Observation questions

- Do children enjoy rolling down a hill?
- Can they talk about speed and height?

➕ Health & Safety

Check the area carefully for any potential hazards. Be aware that some children, e.g. those with severe hay fever, may prefer not to roll in the grass.

What to do:

1. Before the session, locate a gentle grassy slope (not too steep!). Check the area carefully for any potential hazards such as rocks, litter or excrement. If you are unsure, lay down a large tarpaulin cover on the hill.

2. Discuss safety first and decide together on some rules, e.g. only one person can go down the slope at a time.

3. Invite the children to take turns rolling down the hill from top to bottom.

4. Celebrate as each child reaches the bottom of the slope.

Silly dance

Moving to music is enjoyable and fun

What you need:

- Music

What's in it for the children?

Listening to music and making up silly dances is fun for children. Children can be present and in the moment when they are dancing. This activity enables them to let go and enjoy themselves, releasing any worries or negative thoughts. Being allowed to be silly and funny frees up children's imaginations and lets them be who they are.

Taking it forward

- Children could put on a dance show.
- They could make tickets for their show.

Observation questions

- Can children move to music?
- Can children talk about how music makes them feel?

What to do:

1. Talk to the children about music and dance. Do they have a favourite song or dance routine?

2. Put some music on. Ask them, 'How does the music make you feel?' and 'How can you move your body to the music?'.

3. Encourage them to dance freely and to be really 'in the moment' with their dancing, rather than being worried about what others are doing.

4. Invite the children to make up a silly dance.

5. Don't forget to join in with this activity and show your silly side too!

Throwing and catching
Exercising for physical wellbeing

What you need:
- Balls in a variety of sizes

What to do:
1. Ask the children to get into pairs and give each pair a ball.

2. Encourage them to play a game of catch. They should gently throw the ball between themselves and try to catch it.

3. Depending on the age and stage of the children, it may be better to start with the children very close together. To increase the challenge, ask them to move further apart or use smaller balls.

4. Invite them to create their own throwing and catching games and share with the wider group.

What's in it for the children?
Throwing and catching is a good skill to learn in the early years. Throwing and catching a ball is good exercise for a child and it develops important skills such as coordination, aim, taking turns and resilience. Mastering a skill makes children feel good about themselves and to be proud of what they can do.

Taking it forward
- Children could make up their own throwing and catching game.
- They could aim a ball into hoops or buckets.

Observation questions
- Can children throw and catch a ball?
- Can children take turns?
- Can children persevere with something they find difficult?

Wash day

Sensory play with a practical application

What you need:

- Two large bowls
- Soapy water
- Dolls' clothes or baby clothes
- Clean water
- Pegs
- A washing line at child's height

What to do:

1. Fill a bowl with warm soapy water.
2. Invite the children to add some doll or baby clothes to the water.
3. Model how to wash the items in the water and allow the children to have a go.
4. Squeeze out excess water and rinse in a bowl of clean water.
5. Ask the children to peg the clothes on a washing line. Discuss how long they think the washing will take to dry.

What's in it for the children?

Children enjoy mimicking adults and helping to do 'grown up' jobs. Helping out supports a feeling of responsibility and makes others feel cared for and valued. Water play, especially in warm, bubbly water, is soothing and enjoyable and can make children feel happy and calm.

Taking it forward

- Children could wash all sorts of different items.
- They could help an adult with the washing up.
- Children could investigate how much washing up liquid or bubble bath is needed to make various quantities of bubbles.

Observation questions

- Do children talk about capacity (full and empty)?
- Do children like to help?
- Can children talk about what the water feels like?

➕ Health & Safety

Check for any skin allergies before organising this activity.

Yoga

A healthy activity for body and mind

What you need:

- Mats
- Comfortable clothes

What to do:

1. Give each child a mat and ask them to find a space and lay it on the floor. Ensure that everyone is wearing comfortable clothes.

2. Ask the children to take three deep breaths.

3. Model the activity for the children first.

4. Put your feet together and raise both arms in the air. Put your palms together. Hold this position for 15 seconds and then return to a neutral position with your hands by your sides. Repeat this movement three times.

5. Try to touch your toes and push your bottom into the air. Bend your knees if you like. Look down. Hold this position for 15 seconds and then return to a neutral position. Repeat this movement three times.

6. Invite the children to have a go at the same exercises while you continue to model and talk through what you're doing.

7. Ask the children to take another three deep breaths.

8. After the activity, ask the children to sit on their mats and discuss how they feel. How do their bodies feel when they stretch? How do their bodies feel when they breathe deeply and slowly?

What's in it for the children?

Yoga incorporates stretches and deep breathing techniques which calm the mind and body. Doing some simple yoga moves encourages children to breathe, relax and become calm. The physical activity and stretching creates a feeling of wellbeing and the deep breathing calms and soothes the mind.

Taking it forward

- Children could incorporate yoga moves into their daily routine.
- Children could teach others some yoga moves.
- They could play relaxing music while doing yoga.

Observation questions

- Can children follow instructions?
- Can children copy simple yoga moves?

Building

Raise self-esteem through simple construction tasks

What you need:

- Small wooden blocks
- Sticks
- Cotton reels

What to do:

1. Ask the children to think of a time when they have felt proud of themselves. What were they doing? What did they accomplish that made them feel proud?

2. Gather some wooden blocks, sticks and cotton reels.

3. Challenge the children to build things with the objects, e.g. a bridge, a tower, a boat, a city, a zoo. Encourage them to be thoughtful about the process and ask enquiring questions such as 'What materials do you need?' and 'How can you make your model strong so it doesn't fall down?'.

4. Add further challenges, e.g. can you build something tall? Can you build something wide?

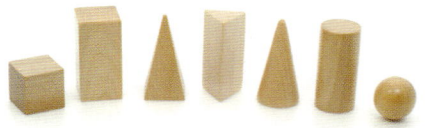

What's in it for the children?

Children enjoy building; it is a satisfying activity with a finished outcome at the end. Setting the children challenges encourages them to use their creative skills, imagination and critical thinking. Building can also develop teamwork and collaboration skills. Success in this simple activity can help to raise self-esteem and encourage children to set higher expectations and challenges for themselves.

Taking it forward

- Children could have building competitions where they set each other challenges.

- Ask the children to work in pairs. One child could have a picture of a simple building, bridge or tower and they have to explain to their partner how to build it.

Observation questions

- Can children work as a team?

- Can children challenge themselves?

- Can children use their critical thinking skills to find solutions to problems?

Colour telescope

Build confidence by designing a toy

What you need:

- Cardboard tubes
- Patterned paper
- Felt tips
- Crayons
- Sticky back plastic
- Tissue paper
- Sequins
- Glitter

What to do:

1. Allow time for every child to decorate a cardboard tube using patterned paper, felt tips and crayons.

2. Cut a circle of sticky back plastic just a bit larger than the end of the tube.

3. Encourage the children to place small bits of coloured tissue paper, sequins and glitter on the sticky back plastic.

4. Stick the circle onto the end of the tube.

5. Model how to hold the colour telescope up to the light and rotate the tube to see the different colours and patterns.

6. Invite the children to talk about and draw the patterns they can see.

What's in it for the children?

These colour telescopes are similar to kaleidoscopes. Kaleidoscopes have been around for many years, providing lots of fun for children. The colours and shapes with the light shining through make interesting patterns. Children will enjoy making their own colour telescope and investigating pattern, and they will feel pride at having made their own toy.

Taking it forward

- Try out different colours and materials to make different patterns.

Observation questions

- Can children create patterns?
- Can children talk about the patterns they make?

Cosy bedtime

Feel safe and loved

What you need:

- Quiet indoor space
- Cushions
- Blankets
- Teddy bears
- Storybook

What's in it for the children?

Children like to be warm and cosy, it makes them feel safe and secure. By making their own snuggly bed children feel a sense of ownership as well as comfort. Cuddling with a favourite teddy and book calms and soothes young children.

Taking it forward

- Children could make a special bed outside on a fine day where they can listen to the leaves and the birds and spend time daydreaming.
- Children could make a hammock with some help from a grown up.
- Children could look at pictures and photographs of beds in different, interesting places, e.g. treehouse, igloo.

Observation questions

- Can children make a cosy bed?
- Can they use appropriate resources and materials?
- Can children talk about their bedtime routine?
- Are children interested in beds in interesting places or other cultures?

What to do:

1. Use this activity before naptime in your setting, or encourage the children to use it as part of their play with dolls or teddies.

2. Find a quiet cosy corner.

3. Invite the children to each choose a cushion and a blanket. Encourage them to set up a 'bed' in the cosy corner and snuggle with a favourite teddy.

4. Discuss their different bedtime routines at home. How does bedtime work in their house? What is their favourite bedtime story? Tell stories about your own bedtime routine too.

5. Choose a well-loved storybook and softly read to the children. Exaggerate a yawn and pretend to slowly drift off to sleep.

Happy photographs

Take photographs of the things that make you happy

What you need:

- Digital camera

What to do:

1. Give a small group of children a digital camera to take photographs of things which make them happy.

2. Over the course of the day, remind the children to take photographs if they particularly enjoy an activity or an interaction with a friend.

3. Sit down as a group and look at all the photographs. Invite the children to talk about what is in each photograph and why it makes them happy.

What's in it for the children?

Talking about things that make you happy and why they make you happy brings smiles and joy. This activity focusses on positive things rather than negative. It supports happiness and emotional wellbeing.

Taking it forward

- Photographs could be printed out and the children could make a collage or a special book (see next idea).

- Children could write captions to go with each photograph.

Observation questions

- Can children talk about what makes them happy?

- Can children use technology for a purpose?

Happy collage

Display happiness for the world to see

What you need:

- Magazines
- Photographs
- Scissors
- Large piece of cardboard
- Glue

What to do:

1. Invite the children to look through magazines and photographs and choose images which make them feel happy. Prompt them with questions such as 'What are your favourite things?', 'What are your favourite colours?' and 'How do these colours make you feel?'.

2. Encourage the children to cut out the images and arrange them on a large piece of cardboard.

3. Once they are happy with the composition, allow them to stick down the photographs and clippings with glue.

4. Make a display of the happy collage pictures.

What's in it for the children?

Children will feel happy looking through favourite photographs and pictures they like. Creating a collage picture will be satisfying and children will feel a sense of achievement and ownership when it is completed and displayed.

Taking it forward

- Children could create 'mood boards' using colours and photographs evoking a particular emotion or mood. They could then talk about those feelings.

Observation questions

- Can children talk about their favourite things and activities which make them happy?

- Can children talk about different feelings?

I am special
A self-esteem boost

What you need:
- A large sheet of paper
- Marker pens

What's in it for the children?
It is nice for children to listen to others talk about their strengths and qualities; it boosts their self-esteem. By writing them down for everyone to see, children can feel proud of themselves. They will feel secure in who they are through this activity. They will also learn that it feels good to say kind things about others.

Taking it forward
- Children could do this activity independently in small groups, using teamwork to complete the task.
- You could draw round each child's hands and do a similar activity. These could then go into a special book that children could look through independently.

Observation questions
- Can children talk about others in positive ways?
- Can they talk about qualities which make people special?
- Can they listen to what others have to say?

What to do:
1. Lay a large sheet of paper on the ground.
2. Choose a child to focus on for this activity. Invite them to lay down on their back and ask them to be as still as they can.
3. Draw around the child with a marker pen, then let the child stand up.
4. Discuss in a small group all the things that make the child special. Prompt the children with questions such as 'What makes them special?' and 'What do they do that is kind or caring?'. Encourage children to talk about personality qualities rather than appearance as these are more important.
5. Act as scribe for the children and write down anything the children say around the edge of the outline.
6. Let the children colour in and decorate the body and display it for all to see.
7. Choose a new child to focus on each week.

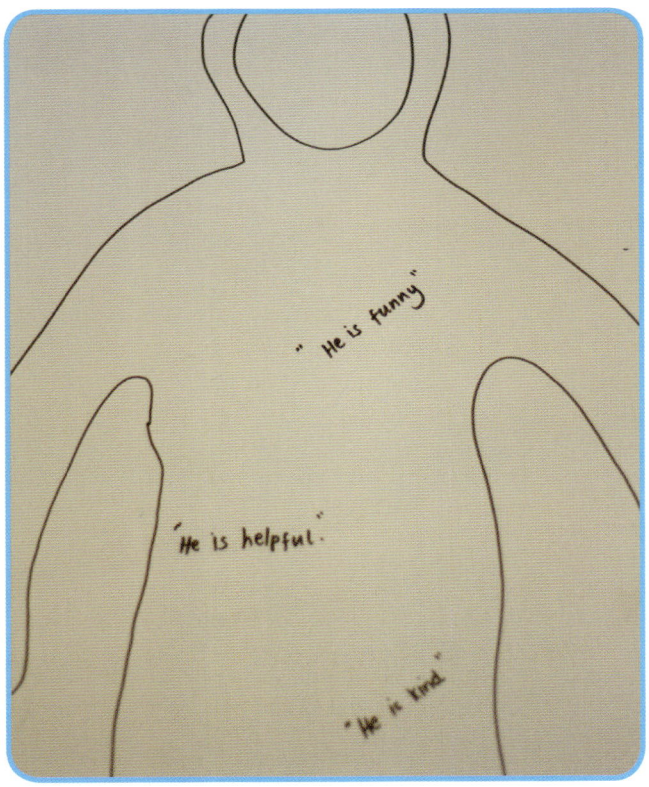

Large scale painting

Be bold and imaginative

What you need:

- Music
- Large piece of paper
- Outdoor space
- Aprons
- Paint
- Large paintbrushes

What to do:

1. Play some music in the background for inspiration and relaxation. Talk with the children about painting and encourage them to discuss whether they like painting and why.

2. Roll out a large sheet of paper in a large outdoor space.

3. Ask the children to put on aprons.

4. Invite them to paint patterns and pictures using big sweeping brush strokes. Reassure them that there is no right or wrong painting and encourage them to be bold in their brush strokes.

5. Suggest that they could paint in time to the music, changing direction or movement as the music changes.

What's in it for the children?

Painting can be therapeutic for children, but some are intimidated by it. Painting on a large scale takes away the pressure to keep within lines or to have very good fine motor skills. The bigger movements the better when painting on a large scale. The physical movement of arm, hand and wrist, as well as the sensory nature of the paint, help children to feel happy, satisfied and content.

Taking it forward

- Children could paint using different tools, e.g. sticks, scrubbing brushes, decorating brushes.
- Sand could be added to the paint to create a different texture.

Observation questions

- Can children use tools to paint on a large scale?
- Do children have good gross and fine motor skills?
- Can children create patterns, textures and designs using their imagination?

Outdoor story time

An opportunity to engage with nature

What you need:

- Outdoor space
- Blanket
- Cushions
- Storybook

What to do:

1. Find a nice comfortable spot under a tree.

2. Lay down a blanket and cushions if the surface is rough.

3. Invite the children to join you on the blanket. Allow them time to get into a comfortable position, either laying down, leaning against the tree or sitting up.

4. Tell them that you will read them a story. They should listen to the story, but they can also think about what they feel, see, hear and smell at the same time.

5. Read them a storybook. This activity works especially well if you choose a story that is set outside, e.g. *We're Going on a Bear Hunt* by Michael Rosen and Helen Oxenbury or *Rosie's Walk* by Pat Hutchins.

6. Encourage the children to take turns telling their own stories from memory or imagination.

What's in it for the children?

Story time is one of the simplest and most enjoyable activities to do with children. Most love listening to stories and it is even better outside! It feels entirely different from listening to stories in the classroom. Children can explore their imaginations as they listen to the story. Being immersed in nature, listening to the leaves rustling on the trees and sounds in the environment can boost children's awareness of their environment, prompt questions and discussion and engage all the senses.

Taking it forward

- Children could find objects in the environment and make up their own stories with props from nature.

Observation questions

- Can children listen to and follow stories?

- Can they make links between stories and real-life experiences?

- Can children make up their own stories?

- Can children talk about the things they see, feel, hear and smell?

Singing show

Bring happiness through song

What you need:

- Crates or wooden blocks
- Familiar music
- Toy microphone

What to do:

1. Make a stage from crates or wooden blocks.
2. Gather the group together in front of the stage.
3. Talk about songs and how they make us feel. Ask the children about their favourite songs? Why do they like their favourite song so much? What other songs do they know?
4. Invite the children to make up their own songs.
5. Put some music on.
6. As a group, sing along to the music.
7. Invite the children to take it in turns to sing on the stage with the toy microphone while their friends watch.

What's in it for the children?

Singing along to music is enjoyable for children. It releases tension and creates happiness. Children will gain confidence and build self-esteem through role play and singing in front of a group.

Taking it forward

- Children could put out chairs and make tickets for the show.
- There could be a panel of judges who give out scores and positive comments.

Observation questions

- Can children sing familiar songs?
- Can they make up their own songs?
- Can children sing with music?
- Are children confident enough to talk and sing in front of a group?

Teddy's day out

Showing love and affection for a favourite toy

What you need:

- Favourite teddy bear

What to do:

1. Ask the children to bring their favourite teddy bear into the setting.

2. At circle time or in small groups, ask the children to introduce their teddy to the group.

3. Prompt them with questions such as 'Who is your special toy?', 'Where did it come from?', 'How old is it?' and 'Can you tell me three facts about it?'.

What's in it for the children?

Most children have a favourite teddy bear or soft toy which they sleep with at night. These toys are comforting and they have usually been with the child since they were very young. Showing it to their friends and special adults and talking about it can help children develop confidence speaking in front of a group as well as making them feel safe and secure.

Taking it forward

- Children could dress up their teddy in different clothes for various adventures.

Observation questions

- Do children have a special soft toy?

- Can they talk about their special toy?

- Can children remember two or three facts about their toy?

- Can children talk in front of a group?

Time for toast

Learning to care for yourself and others

What you need:

- Slices of bread
- Toaster
- Plates
- Butter
- Butter knives

What to do:

1. Talk to the children about what they like to eat for breakfast or for a snack. Suggest that sometimes we receive or give food as an act of nurture. Tell them that you are going to be making toast together.

2. Working in pairs, give each child a slice of bread and help them to pop the bread in the toaster.

3. Let the pair decide which child will push the plunger.

4. When the toast pops up, get it out carefully and place each piece on a plate to give to the children.

5. Invite them to butter their toast.

6. Cut the toast into halves or quarters and encourage them to sit down to eat with friends.

What's in it for the children?

By making their own toast (if age appropriate), children feel a sense of responsibility and trust. They are gaining valuable life skills and they are learning how to look after themselves and others. Caring for others and learning new skills leads to a sense of wellbeing.

Taking it forward

- Children could learn how to make a variety of simple snacks to share with others.
- Children could write a menu for their friends to choose from.

Observation questions

- Can children take responsibility for themselves?
- Can children stay safe with support from a grown up?
- Can children follow instructions?

 Health & Safety
Check for any food allergies before you start the activity.

Card making

Encourage kindness through creativity

What you need:

- A4 card in various colours
- Felt-tip pens
- Crayons
- Glitter
- Sequins
- Glue

What to do:

1. Discuss with the children any cards that they have recently sent or received. These might be birthday cards, new home cards or Christmas cards, for example.

2. Explain that to receive a card means that you have been in someone's thoughts and to give a card means that you care for that person.

3. Give each child a piece of A4 card. Depending on the age and stage of the children, either model how to fold a piece of card in half or prepare the folded cards in advance.

4. Explain that they are going to create a card for a friend. Ask them questions as they play, e.g. 'Who are you going to give your card to?' and 'What kind thing has someone done for you?'.

5. Invite the children to decorate their cards using felt-tip pens, crayons, glitter, sequins and glue.

6. Encourage them to write a message inside to a friend to make them smile.

7. Let the children give their card to a friend.

What's in it for the children?

Giving and receiving cards is fun and brings a lot of happiness. Making a card, putting thought, time and love into it, and giving it to someone you care for is even better! This activity is a good way of teaching children that kindness and making others smile is important.

Taking it forward

- Children could make a collection of cards to give out to friends and family members.

Observation questions

- Can children use their imagination and creative skills to make a card?

- Can children write a simple sentence or caption inside the card?

- Do children enjoy giving and receiving cards?

- Do children understand the concept of kindness?

Gift box

Learn to show care for others

What you need:

- Small boxes with lids, one per child
- Felt-tip pens
- Paint
- Tissue paper
- PVA glue
- Paintbrushes
- Paper
- Pens

What to do:

1. Discuss the idea that everyone is special to someone. Talk with the children about who is special to them, e.g. a good friend, a parent or a grandparent perhaps.

2. Give each child a small box with a lid.

3. Invite them to decorate their boxes using felt-tip pens, paint or tissue paper and glue.

4. Encourage them to write or draw a note to a friend, fold up and place inside the box.

5. Give your gift box to a friend.

What's in it for the children?

Giving gifts to others is enjoyable, especially when it is something you have thought carefully about and made yourself. Children will enjoy giving their gift box to someone special and they will get a sense of happiness and wellbeing from creating it themselves.

Taking it forward

- Children could leave clues in boxes for their friends to find and they could go on a treasure hunt.

Observation questions

- Do children enjoy making gift boxes for their friends?
- Can children talk about what makes their friend special?

Listening to the birds

Calm down with nature sounds

What you need:

- A place near some trees
- Your ears

What's in it for the children?

Encouraging children to be still and to listen carefully is beneficial, supporting the development of attention and listening skills. Being outside amongst nature is grounding and calming. Listening to bird song can create a sense of wellbeing and contentment.

Taking it forward

- This activity also works well at the beach, listening to the waves, or in the woods on a breezy day, listening to the leaves rustling in the trees.
- Children could draw or write the things they can hear.

Observation questions

- Can children tune in to the sounds?
- Can children maintain attention?
- Can children describe the sounds they hear?

What to do:

1. Discuss how we might feel when we have lots of worries inside us or when there are lots of noise and distractions that overwhelm us. Talk about some solutions to these feelings, such as speaking to an adult or spending some time in the quiet corner. Suggest that sometimes nature can help us to feel calm.

2. Go for a walk somewhere where there are trees, flowers, birds and wild animals.

3. Invite the children to settle in a circle. Encourage them to listen carefully and tune into the sounds of the birds in the trees and the rustle of leaves.

4. Encourage them to close their eyes, be quiet and focus all their attention on the sounds they can hear. Ask them questions such as 'What can you hear?', 'What does it sound like?' and 'How many sounds can you hear?'.

Minibeast stone painting

Create resources to encourage social interaction

What you need:

- Smooth stones or pebbles
- Paint
- Paintbrushes
- Outdoor space
- Photographs or drawings of minibeasts
- Varnish

What's in it for the children?

In this activity children will be using their sense of touch, feeling the textures of the stones and pebbles. By painting their stone, they will be using their imagination and creativity which contributes to feelings of wellbeing. Hiding their stones and playing games with them encourages social interaction which helps to develop a positive self-image.

Taking it forward

- Children could make a collection of minibeasts to make a minibeast family.
- Children could hide their stones around the outdoor area for their friends to find.
- Children could write kind messages on the stones for their friends.
- Children could tell stories using their stones.

Observation questions

- Are the children engaged in their activity?
- Do they maintain attention until the task is complete?

What to do:

1. Gather a selection of smooth stones or pebbles. Wash and thoroughly dry them to remove any dirt that might prevent the paint from sticking.

2. Set out paints and brushes in an outdoor space, and provide photographs or drawings of minibeasts as inspiration.

3. Invite the children to choose a stone. Encourage them to hold the stone gently and examine it carefully. How does it feel?

4. Ask them to paint a minibeast on one side of their stone, choosing colours carefully.

5. Encourage them to listen to the sounds in the environment as they work.

6. Once the children have finished painting, varnish the stones for them.

7. When the stones are completely dry, tell the children that they are going to play a game.

8. Let them choose a quiet space outside to place the stone. Play a game of 'find the stones' where each child has to find a stone belonging to someone else.

Post a compliment
Make others feel valued and loved

What you need:

- Shoe box
- Red paint
- Scissors
- Notecards
- Pens
- Post box

What's in it for the children?

It is always nice to give and receive compliments; it makes people feel special. Saying nice things about a person can have a positive effect on their self-image and self-esteem, especially when compliments are focussed on personality and actions rather than appearance. Children will enjoy posting their compliments and then having them read out or shared with others.

Taking it forward

- Children could draw a picture for a friend if they cannot yet write.
- Discussion could be opened up around 'random acts of kindness'.
- Compliments could be displayed and talk could centre around how compliments make people feel.

Observation questions

- Do children know what a compliment is?
- Can children give each other compliments?
- Can children talk about how compliments make them feel?

What to do:

1. Before the session, cover an old shoe box in red paint. Cut a hole in the top and decorate accordingly.

2. Ask the children if they have ever received a compliment and what it was for. Talk about how compliments make people feel valued and loved. Tell them that they will be writing or drawing compliments for others today.

3. Give each child a notecard. Encourage them to think about a good friend and write or draw a compliment about them. Prompt them with questions such as 'How is your friend special?' and 'What do they do that is kind?'.

4. Ask the children to write their friend's name at the top and sign their own name at the bottom. An adult can act as scribe for the children if required.

5. Encourage the children to post their notecards in a post box.

6. Each day, draw out a new notecard from the post box and discuss who it is for and why.

Plant a seed

Nurture a plant

What you need:

- Soil
- Small plant pot, one per child
- Seeds
- Water

What to do:

1. Discuss how living things grow. Link this discussion to the children's own growth and how they have changed from being a baby. Tell them that they will be caring for and nurturing a plant from a seed.

2. Model how to plant a seed before allowing the children to each plant their own seed.

3. Put some soil into a plant pot. Compact the soil lightly with the back of your hand.

4. Make a small hole in the centre with your finger.

5. Push in the seed and cover it with soil.

6. Water it.

7. Invite the children to plant their own seeds.

8. Watch the seeds grow over the following weeks.

What's in it for the children?

Children will feel a sense of pride and satisfaction from planting and growing a plant from a tiny seed, leading to a sense of wellbeing. They will talk about how to look after and nurture their seed. This can also be a sensory experience; children will be able to enjoy the sensation of the soil falling through their fingers.

Taking it forward

- Children could design and make a label for their plant.

- Children could keep a diary, recording what has happened to the plant each day.

Observation questions

- Are the children able to talk about growth and change?

- Can they care for a plant over time?

Barefoot walk

A sensory experience to promote connection with nature

What you need:

- Grass
- Water pool
- Soil
- Sand tray
- Stone or concrete path

What's in it for the children?

Going on a barefoot walk is a valuable sensory experience for young children. They can tune in to how materials feel on their skin as they walk. Not only is it enjoyable, it is also a fun activity to do with friends. The sensation of the different materials on their skin may be calming for some children or challenging for others.

Taking it forward

- Children could read the story *We're Going on a Bear Hunt* by Michael Rosen and Helen Oxenbury before they go on their barefoot walk.

- Children could design their own 'silly' barefoot walk using slime, shaving foam.

Observation questions

- Can children talk about how the surfaces differ?

- Can children talk about how each material feels?

What to do:

1. Ideally, set up this activity outdoors. Ensure that the different surfaces are all easily accessible.

2. Ask the children to take off their shoes and socks. Encourage them to roll up their trousers if necessary.

3. Invite them to walk over the grass, water, soil, sand and stone one at a time, focussing on how each of the surfaces feel underfoot. What does it feel like? How do the sensations differ? Invite discussion and delight by joining in and sharing your experiences too.

4. Ask the children which surface they prefer. Are there any other surfaces they would like to try?

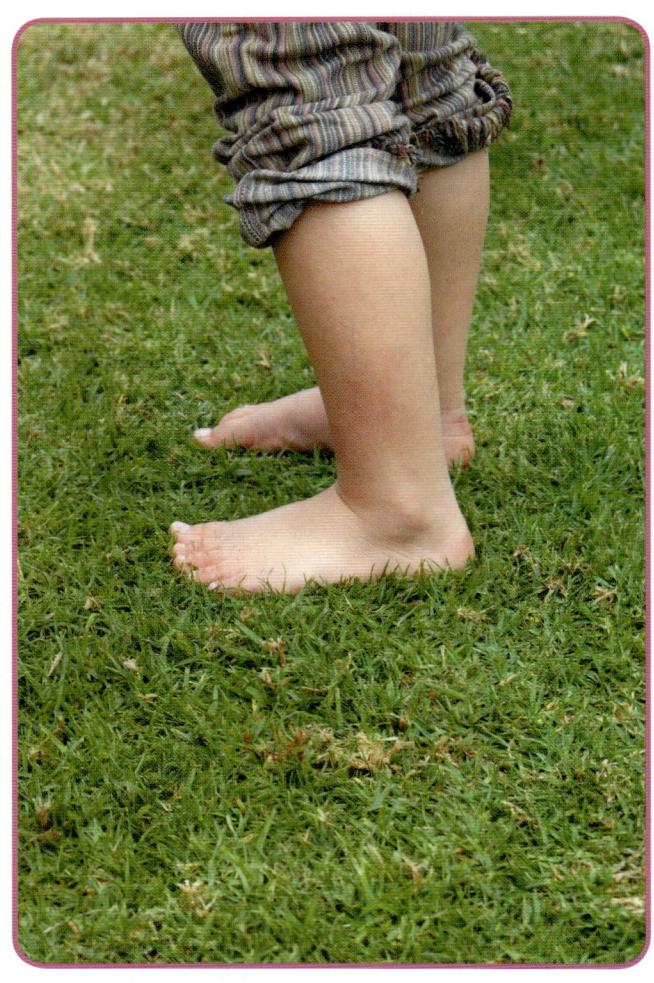

Blow paint

Slow down and relax with careful breathing

What you need:

- Large sheet of paper
- Paint in various colours
- Straws
- Water

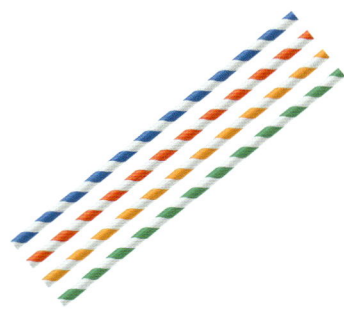

What to do:

1. Lay out a large sheet of paper.
2. Put blobs of different coloured paint on the paper, spaced out so that several children can access the paper at once.
3. Ask the children to gather around the paper and talk about breathing. Practise taking deep breaths. Ask them, 'What does your body feel like when you breathe in?' and 'What does your body feel like when you breathe out?'
4. Give each child a straw and invite them to blow through the straw near to the paint blobs. Explain that it is important to blow the paint and not to suck it.
5. If the paint is too thick to blow, add water to make it runnier. What patterns can they create? Allow the children to access the activity for as long as they like.

What's in it for the children?

Focussing carefully on their breath enables children to empty their minds and centre themselves. To effectively blow the paint through the straw requires a child to take deep breaths. Taking deep breaths calms the mind and body. Creating patterns and engaging in a fun activity creates a feeling of contentment.

Taking it forward

- Children could add glitter or water to the paint to change the outcome.
- They could talk about how changing the consistency of the paint affects how hard they have to blow through the straw.

Observation questions

- Can children focus on their breathing?
- Can children talk about how their body feels?
- Do children talk about their feelings?

Clay animals

Create new animal friends

What to do:

1. Set up individual stations for the number of children in your group. Ensure each station has a lump of clay and the tools are within easy reach.

2. Invite the children to explore the clay. Ask them questions, e.g. 'What does the clay feel like?'.

3. Model how to warm and soften the clay by rolling it in your hands.

4. Suggest that the children could create an animal out of the clay. Ask them what animal they would like to make.

5. Encourage them to think creatively about how they can represent different features, e.g. eyes, fur or claws.

6. Provide buttons for eyes, matchsticks for spikes, etc. but do not insist the children use them.

What's in it for the children?

Clay is an excellent sensory material. Modelling with clay can be soothing as it is cool and smooth. Creating something out of clay which will dry hard is satisfying. The act of creating a model from clay can be calming as well as satisfying, and children may feel a sense of accomplishment.

Taking it forward

- Children could agree to make a group of animals, e.g. woodland animals.
- Children could use small world resources to make a background scene for their animals to be displayed in.

Observation questions

- Can children mould the clay to make a model?
- Can children describe the way it feels?
- Can children design and adapt their model as they go along?

Cloud spotting
Be still and calm

What you need:

- Outdoor space
- Blanket
- Cushions
- Sunglasses
- A clear day

What's in it for the children?

Children can take time out of their busy, action-packed day to lay still and quiet outside, allowing themselves to focus on the sky and the clouds. Watching clouds move, shift and change can be very calming and can help to soothe the mind.

Taking it forward

- Children could make up stories about the shapes and objects they see in the clouds.
- Children could make cloud pictures using paint, cotton wool, shaving foam, etc.
- This activity may lead to discussions about weather or space.

Observation questions

- Can children talk about the things they see, hear, smell and feel?

✚ Health & Safety

Ensure children always wear sunglasses with good UVA protection when looking at the sky, especially on a bright sunny day. Don't look at the sky for long periods of time as it can damage your eyes.

What to do:

1. Find a nice comfortable spot outside.
2. Spread out a large blanket and scatter cushions around.
3. Ask each child to put on a pair of sunglasses and join you on the blanket.
4. Encourage the children to lay down on their backs and look up at the sky.
5. Suggest that the children close their eyes. Ask them questions such as 'What can you hear?', 'What can you smell?' and 'What can you feel as you lay here on the blanket?'.
6. Encourage the children to slowly open their eyes and look at the sky. What shapes or objects can they spot in the clouds?
7. There is no right or wrong answer when watching clouds so ensure that all ideas are given credit. Let their imaginations run wild!

Make-believe creatures

Roll, knead and stretch

What you need:

- Dough
- Matchsticks
- Sequins
- Buttons

What to do:

1. Invite the children to knead the dough to warm it up. Encourage them to talk about the texture of the dough and what they like or don't like about it. Does it feel different once it has warmed up?

2. Talk about the minibeasts and creatures that the children know. Suggest that they could make creatures based on their imagination rather than on real life. Explore what the imaginary creatures might look like.

3. Allow them to roll the dough into the shape of the creature they want to make. Ask questions as they play, e.g. 'How many eyes will it have?' and 'What colours will you use and why?'.

4. Encourage them to push matchsticks, sequins and buttons into the dough to add detail to the creature.

5. Participate in the play and make your own creature. Make up a little story as you make the creatures together.

What's in it for the children?

Children will be able to enjoy the sensory activity of kneading and rolling the dough, and feeling the texture. This sensory experience can be soothing for children and the repetitive tasks of rolling and kneading can be calming too. Children will get a sense of accomplishment from creating something out of the dough which contributes to their overall sense of wellbeing.

Taking it forward

- Children could make more dough creatures to create a family.

- Children could make up stories about the creatures and tell them to their friends.

Observation questions

- Are the children showing high levels of involvement?

- Can they talk about texture?

Magic potion making

Scents to distract from distress

What you need:

- Selection of herbs, flowers and spices, e.g. lavender, rosemary, thyme, daisies, mint
- Scissors
- Warm water
- Pots of different sizes
- Wooden spoons

What's in it for the children?

Children will be able to focus their minds on the activity using their sense of smell. Calming herbs such as lavender can be used. By becoming involved in the physical sensations of smelling, touching, snipping and mixing, children's minds will be distracted from any negative thoughts. They will get a sense of pride and accomplishment from creating a potion with herbs.

Taking it forward

- Children could label their potions, making up imaginative names.
- Children could discuss their potion making with others.
- Children could talk about the unique characteristics of different herbs.

Observation questions

- Are the children showing high levels of involvement?
- Can they talk about their likes and dislikes?

What to do:

1. Set out a large selection of herbs in an accessible area of the provision. Think carefully about the herbs you offer; lavender is known to have a calming effect and mint is fresh and can help you to think clearly.

2. Invite the children to sniff the herbs. Talk about the different smells and compare them. Use questions such as 'Do they smell different or similar?', 'How do the smells make you feel?' and 'What do the herbs feel like?' to prompt discussion.

3. Suggest that the children could cut small bits from herb leaves.

4. Provide warm water, pots and wooden spoons to facilitate potion making with the herbs that have been explored. Encourage the children to focus their attention on the repetitive actions of stirring and mixing to soothe their minds.

5. As the children play, talk about what the potion could be for.

+ Health & Safety

Check for allergies before providing lavender or other herbs.

Mindfulness colouring

Focus the mind to stay within the lines

What you need:

- Mindfulness colouring sheets
- Coloured pencils
- Paints
- Crayons
- Felt-tip pens

What to do:

1. Provide the children with a variety of colouring worksheets to choose from; you can find many available online for free. Mandalas and other repeating patterns can work well, but simple scenes or animals are also a good choice.

2. Set out a range of art supplies to cater for the desires and needs of all the children. Include coloured pencils, paints, crayons and felt-tip pens.

3. Invite the children to choose their colouring sheet and get stuck in. Work alongside them – take your time and enjoy colouring in!

What's in it for the children?

Lots of children (and adults) enjoy colouring in. It is a calming activity and the repetitive action of the pencil strokes is soothing. When children focus on the colouring and keeping within the lines, it enables them to be present in the moment, free from worries or negative thoughts.

Taking it forward

- Children could colour a variety of different designs and display them for others to see.

- Children could stick to similar colours for each design (for example, cool blue colours for one sheet and warm pink and red colours for another).

Observation questions

- Can children talk about colours and shades?

- Can children sort colours into groups (cool colours, warm colours)?

- Can children maintain attention?

Noodle fun!

A focus on touch

What you need:

- Tuff tray
- Warm, cooked noodles

What to do:

1. Set up a tuff tray full of warm, cooked noodles.

2. Invite the children to put their hands in and play with the noodles. Encourage them to squish, roll, pat and pour them.

3. Ask them questions to prompt discussion, such as:

   a. What do the noodles feel like?

   b. Can you describe the texture?

   c. Do you like the feel of them?

   d. What do you like about it?

4. Allow the children time to access and explore the materials independently.

What's in it for the children?

Sensory activities can support wellbeing because they encourage children to focus their attention on their sense of touch. Soft textures, like noodles, can be pleasurable for children. Others may not like the soft textures so may prefer dry materials like rice or lentils.

Taking it forward

- Children could explore a range of different foods and textures.
- They could develop their vocabulary and explanation skills by talking about textures with others.

Observation questions

- Do children enjoy the sensory experience?
- Can children talk about textures and sensations?
- Can children talk about their likes and dislikes?

Perfume making

Soothing scents to relax with

What you need:

- Flower petals or cherry blossom
- Tuff tray
- Herbs, e.g. thyme, mint, rosemary
- Lavender
- Pots and pans
- Lukewarm water
- Mixing spoons
- Strainers

What to do:

1. When flowers or blossom are in abundance, encourage the children to go outside and gather fallen flower petals from around the setting.

2. Set up a tuff tray ready for when the children return with their scavenger hunt. Provide herbs, lavender and other flowers that the children may not have been able to find outdoors. Set out pots and pans, along with lukewarm water, mixing spoons and strainers.

3. Invite the children to mix the petals with some water until the scent from the petals makes a special perfume. Allow time for them to access the activity for as long as they're interested.

What's in it for the children?

Scent is powerful in that it can bring back memories and emotions. Lots of children enjoy making their own perfume from flower petals and herbs. The stirring action involved in mixing the perfume is repetitive and soothing.

Taking it forward

- Children could use different petals and herbs to make a variety of perfumes.
- Children may like to label their perfumes, thinking of unusual names.

Observation questions

- Can children talk about the scents they smell?
- Can children maintain attention and use their imagination to create a perfume?

✚ Health & Safety

Check the outdoor setting for potential hazards before allowing the children to collect flowers or blossom. Check for allergies before providing lavender or other herbs.

Water play

Calming and soothing play with water

What you need:

- Water tray or large bowls
- Water
- Bubble bath
- Food colouring
- Pans
- Jugs
- Bottles
- Whisks
- Spoons
- Pipettes

What to do:

1. Fill a water tray or some large bowls with water.
2. Add bubble bath and food colouring.
3. Allow the children time to enjoy pouring, squirting and stirring the water using the resources provided.
4. Ask questions about their play, e.g. 'What are you doing?' and 'What are you making?'. Encourage investigation with prompts such as 'What will happen if you stir or pour the water with this resource?'.

What's in it for the children?

Water play is a sensory experience that most young children enjoy. They naturally like to pour and move water between containers. When the water is enticing with bubbles and colours and interesting resources, the play can become more creative and imaginative.

Taking it forward

- Children could investigate capacity, full and empty, using water and containers.

- Children could explore how water changes and alters when mixed with oil or foam.

Observation questions

- Can children talk about actions such as pouring, stirring, whisking?

- Can children use everyday language to talk about capacity, e.g. full, empty?

- Can children make up their own games using water and containers?

✚ Health & Safety

Check for any skin allergies before you start the activity.

Sewing

A repetitive and soothing craft to calm the mind

What you need:

- Binca (cross stitch) fabric
- Plastic sewing needles
- Cotton thread in bright colours

What to do:

1. Give each child a square of cross stitch fabric and a plastic sewing needle.

2. Allow the children to choose their own thread colour.

3. Depending on the age and stage of the children, thread their needles for them or support them to thread their own needles. Ensure that a knot is tied in the end.

4. Model some simple stitches and then invite the children to think about what patterns they could make. Give them freedom to craft as they like.

What's in it for the children?

Sewing can be a therapeutic activity; it enables children to focus on one thing and zone out any negative thoughts or worries. It requires concentration so develops children's attention skills. Crafting and creating leads to a sense of satisfaction, pride and wellbeing.

Taking it forward

- Children could make little patterns to give to friends and family.

- Sew together all of the squares when finished and hang the quilt as a wall decoration or use it as a blanket.

Observation questions

- Can children concentrate for prolonged periods of time?

- Do children have the fine motor skills to thread a needle, hold it and sew?

- Can children create patterns and talk about them?

Sensory basket

Connect favourite textures with positive feelings

What you need:

- A range of different fabrics and textures
- A basket

What to do:

1. Invite the children to bring in any fabrics that they treasure. This might be a favourite cushion cover, a snippet of fabric from an old bedsheet or similar.

2. You should also provide a range of textured fabric to ensure there is a good variety. Ask local craft clubs to save their scraps for you.

3. Fill a basket with the various fabrics and textures.

4. Invite a small group of children to close their eyes and put their hands into the basket.

5. Talk about the textures they can feel. Ask questions such as 'What does it feel like?', 'What does it make you think of?' and 'How does it make you feel?'.

What's in it for the children?

Children are encouraged to use their sense of touch to feel the fabrics and textures. They can talk about what each piece feels like and how it makes them feel. Some children may link textures to emotions or experiences. Some fabrics and textures can be comforting for children and can help them feel safe, loved and protected.

Taking it forward

- Children could make transient pictures or scenes from the fabrics.

- Photograph the children's work and annotate it with their ideas as a record.

Observation questions

- Can children talk about different textures?

- Can children talk about how different textures make them feel?

Soil and mud play

A sensory activity in nature

What you need:

- Dry soil
- Water
- Watering can
- Small rakes
- Trowels
- Garden forks
- Buckets or pots

What to do:

1. Find a patch of dry soil.

2. Invite the children to put their hands in the soil to feel if it is dry. Encourage them to pick it up and allow it to trickle through their fingers like sand.

3. Add some water from a watering can and ask them to feel the difference. Talk about the change in temperature and texture. Do any minibeasts come out of the soil when you water it?

4. Allow the children time to get their hands in and play with the soil, make mud pies, smooth the soil, rake it, dig and pour using the tools provided.

What's in it for the children?

Children will be able to feel the soil, talking about how dry soil is different to wet soil. They will have the opportunity to play in the soil: building, making, pouring, digging and raking. This tactile experience and being close to nature can nurture a calm sense of wellbeing. Playing outside with nature can be beneficial to children's wellbeing by encouraging a sense of calmness.

Taking it forward

- Children could dig for worms in order to make a wormery which can be taken into the classroom or home for closer examination. Remember though, wormeries need to be kept moist!

Observation questions

- Do the children enjoy the sensation of the soil?
- Can the children change the state of the soil (dry, wet, warm, cold, compact, loose) and talk about these changes?

✚ Health & Safety

Remember to always wash your hands carefully with warm soapy water after handling soil and mud.

Slime play

Pour, squish and stretch your way to wellbeing

What you need:

- 200 ml washable PVA glue
- Bowl
- 1–2 drops liquid food colouring (optional)
- ¼ cup glitter (optional)
- 1 tsp baking soda
- Spoon
- 2–3 tbsp saline solution (i.e. contact lens solution)
- Tuff tray
- Sequins, beans or other small items

What to do:

1. Pour the glue into a bowl and add food colouring and glitter if desired.
2. Add the baking soda and mix with the spoon.
3. Add the saline solution.
4. Mix slowly until a ball of slime forms. Knead the slime until smooth.
5. Put the slime on a tuff tray.
6. Invite the children to put their hands into the slime and push, pull, squish and knead it with their fingers.
7. Encourage them to watch how the slime moves and alters as they play with it.
8. Introduce the additional resources, e.g. sequins, and allow the children to use these freely.

What's in it for the children?

This is an effective sensory activity, encouraging children to hold and feel unusual textures. Slime is easily manipulated and makes interesting shapes. Pouring, squishing and stretching the slime is a tactile experience which can open up discussion about materials and changes. Children will enjoy this activity, feeling the slime slide between their fingers.

Taking it forward

- Children could make their own slime.
- Children could pour the slime between containers.
- Children could put objects in the slime and observe what happens.
- They could use tweezers to pick small objects out of the slime to develop fine motor skills.

Observation questions

- Can children manipulate the slime?
- Can they talk about how the slime feels?
- Can children talk about changes?

Wind chime

Evoke positive feelings and moods in children and adults

What you need:

- Shells
- Drill (optional)
- Basket
- Beads
- Small stick
- String

What to do:

1. Prepare a selection of shells in advance of the activity. Search for shells that naturally have holes in them. Alternatively, use a drill to carefully make holes in the shells.

2. Put the shells in a basket with the beads.

3. Ask the children to help you search the outdoor area for a small but sturdy stick.

4. Tie five or six pieces of string from the stick.

5. Invite the children to help you thread the shells and beads onto the string.

6. Tie the ends of the string securely and hang the wind chime in the outdoor area.

7. Sit with the children beneath the wind chime and enjoy the sound together.

What's in it for the children?

Wind chimes create a relaxing sound in the breeze. Children will enjoy making the wind chime and listening to the gentle sounds. These gentle sounds, drifting on the breeze, can support a feeling of wellbeing.

Taking it forward

- Children could experiment by using different materials and objects to make their wind chime.

- Children could talk about the different sounds they make.

Observation questions

- Can children talk about the sounds they hear?

- Can they create something which makes sounds?